How To Install Kodi On A Fire Stick:

Step-by-Step Guide With Pictures To Master Your Kodi

Table of content

Introduction:

Kodi is an application which is previously called XBMC is the most successful, freely available and open source application media core for enjoying song, videos, photos, games, and many other things. Kodi is runnable on many operating systems such as OS X, Linux, Microsoft windows, iOS, and Android devices, proposing a 10 ft. user interface to be used with remote controls and televisions. It permits its users to play and watch movies, podcasts, music, and different files related to digital media from local as well as community storage media and the web. The Wiki and boards are bursting with the competencies and support for the brand new consumer right as much as the appliance developer. Kodi application also has the valuable Google+, Facebook, Twitter and several YouTube pages.

Kodi application is the platform replacement of the windows Media middle for many home pc for theater purpose (HTPC). It has many types of skins which can be change its interfaces, and have more than a few plug-ins that allow the customers to access streaming media content material through the online services for instance the Amazon high instant Video, Pandora internet Radio, Crackle, Spotify, YouTube and Rhapsody. The later forms have a personal recorder for recording videos, it is called PVR and graphical front finish for receiving are living television with (EPG) electronic program advisor and high definition (DVR) digital video recorder support. Now it only helps the users to stream content to their television through practically internet related device, but also the application is the open source in nature and is highly customizable.

Chapter 01 – Kodi- A Brief Introduction

Kodi is the software which is open source developed certainly for the home entertainment. The application is absolutely free. Despite the fact that it was in the beginning designed for the Microsoft Xbox and referred to as (XBMC) Xbox Media core. The application has been endured to conform and spawning the community.

Despite of many other services such as Plex, Chrome cast or Kodi is maintained by the non-revenue firms usually called the XBMC foundation. However it could be the regularly upgraded and modified through 1000s of coders around the globe. For the production in 2003, Kodi application has been formed by means of more than 450 software designers and developers and about more than 150 translators.

The Kodi application is runnable on computers and residence servers related to huge TVs, Kodi pulls all the content immediately to the front of your room. On the other hand, contemporary community led merchandise mean it would be much viable to run the application on chosen tablets and smartphones.

Kodi application runs on any pc, tablet or smartphone right into a digital set top field or streamer, which usually gives users the capacity to flow documents from the web, a typical home network and storage.

On the other hand, the other TV streamers comparable to the brand new Apple tv, and Amazon fire television Stick, Chrome cast 2, Kodi application might not be held back with the aid of a curated app store or licensing, so it allows the users to download a variety of apps, and watch whatever they like.

The rationale development of Kodi makes the user interface searching by means of the user's content material easy. The application points that the builders call a 10 foot user interface, which means it may be learn from a theoretical point of view up to 10 ft. away and because of this range of developed in programs, the users could be easily browse snap shots, videos, and podcasts rapidly and readily.

What is suitable with Kodi?

Kodi is just about each gadget that the user could feel of. The software media center is much convenient and easy to install and download, and is much suitable with Linux, OS X, windows, Android and also with the Pi microcomputer Raspberry. Those users who are addicted to use the iOS, for them the system is reasonably more problematic: iPhone users must ensure that their mobile phone is jail broken earlier than downloading it.

Is the Kodi application authorized?

The straightforward answer to this question is yes. In the most elementary form, Kodi is a section of streaming application which is surely designed to display content on a variety of instruments, and that suggests it would be perfectly legal for its users.

Nevertheless, same as the browser like torrent client, or any other tool, it would be easy to use Kodi for many dry purposes and less cut.

Streaming and running the add-ons that will let the users to check the range of movies or videos are probably frowned upon; nevertheless it would be much predominant to take into account that it is much identical as utilizing an online browser similar to Chrome or Safari to find a flow for a movie or carrying occasion.

For those users who suspect an add-on presents insurance policy or a movie library which is too just right to be authentic, chances are it on the whole is.

What is Kodi's stance?

As most of the users expect that the developers of Kodi are keen to distance their applications from the world of murky add-ons, and also manage that in its ordinary form, this application is just as legal as the other web browser.

The application Kodi started out existence back in the year of 2003 as homebrew software for the common Xbox, aptly known as (XBMC) Xbox Media Centre, before diverging away from the UI and within the techniques of jogging Android, iOS, BSD, Linux, Microsoft windows, Mac OS X, and others. It has the ability of turning on the computing devices that are runnable for those programs into full-fledged streaming and set-prime bins, with the capability to play the documents having media files saved for your local network, or for home network, and online.

It would be rarely an exotic factor at the present time, but the Kodi stand out from the rest is the true fact that it is an open source application. Whilst the process is maintained by way of the XBMC basis, it would be alternatively exceptional to most of the time each method available in the market. There would not be any licensing concerned and there would be no managed app shops, which means that the community has the ability to increase anything they like. In theory that means the user could watch and hearken to anything you need, while not having to worry about giant organizations like Google tying and Apple matters up with red tape.

This also makes it very general for pirates. However, same as the likes of the software called Bit Torrent, there would be a lot more to Kodi than illegally and freely getting access to copyrighted things. As the user would expect any copyright or illegal infringing content comes from third party, and it would not be much encouraged with the aid of the folks in the back of Kodi.

Chapter 02 – Easy tips and tricks to install Kodi on Amazon Fire Stick

Kodi is the most high quality portions of streaming software in the market place in the present time. Now it only helps the users to stream content to their television through practically any internet related device, however the application is the open source nature method it's infinitely customizable and hence particularly flexible and light weight software. If the user can think of a gadget that the user wish to have to move content material from to your television, probabilities are Kodi will be runnable on it.

Essentially the most standard gadget to get Kodi strolling on is Amazon's television Stick. This most lightweight dongle plugs streaming directly into the television and can be easily slip into the pocket if the user happens to so wish. Mix it with the influence of Kodi, and there may be actually nothing that the user cannot do with it. Hanging Kodi on the Amazon fire television stick would not be as straightforward as putting in Kodi in to the Chrome cast however, we all should be much thankful to ES File Explorer, it would not as hard as the user may also suppose it is.

The Kodi application is runnable on computers and residence servers related to huge TVs, Kodi pulls all the content immediately to the front of your room. On the other hand, contemporary community led merchandise mean it would be much viable to run the application on chosen tablets and smartphones.

Tips to install Kodi on Amazon Fir Stick

1. Uploading Kodi to the users' fire place television Stick permits the users to quite a lot of further content.
2. After that the capacity to run fascinating add-ons – and it best takes a couple of minutes to hook up.

3. To the starting method, customers have got to first circumnavigate to Settings process options.

4. To use Kodi, the user ought to make sure the Apps from the Sources that are eventually unknown are turned ON. This may help the users to run apps from outside the apps of Amazon ecosystem, including Kodi.

5. After completing this, the user would want the file management software, or a technique of manipulating documents to the fire television Stick.

6. The one of the most preferred ones is ES File Explorer, so search for it in the App store before installing and downloading it.

7. In addition to it, being a great method to control local records, ES File Explorer software also makes it feasible to effectively download 1/3 - party content.

8. Navigate to the application to add and the user would be able to offer with a field to fill in.

9. Within the textbox marked named as path, the user just need to enter the next download handle for Kodi downloading website. Then always add the link to the users' favorites.

10. The user have to click on the ARM link once – it would be somewhat easy and comfortable to find, but play around with the cursor and the user will get there with a bit of endurance.

11. When the user have clicked on the link of the ARM nothing will happen – but the user must not be panic, that is totally common.

12. The user just simply have to navigate the users' way to the three dots in the corner of right hand nook, click on it and prefer the tab named open in another new Browser for opening it. This will make an effort to do.

13. As soon as Kodi has downloaded, selected Open File and try to install. A speak box will be shown, inquiring for permission to put in.

14. Go ahead and click to agree to their conditions and install, and then prefer download again.

15. After the user bought Kodi mounted on an the Raspberry Pi 2 and Amazon fire television Stick, the user will have got to join the device of alternative to the HDMI input of their Xbox One as if the user happen to have been linking up a pc to the console.

16. The TV choice on to the Xbox One must now bring up the Raspberry Pi 2 or Amazon fire television Stick interface. Navigate to the application of Kodi application to make use of it. To try this on an Amazon fire television Stick the user will have to go to Settings functions manipulate to established different functions, and then scroll to Kodi.

17. Whenever the user on the Kodi home screen of user interface, use it as the user customarily would (most of the user advisor for that right here). If the user prefer to, that the user could even snap the Kodi video to the monitor even as you play a recreation.

18. Kodi application runs on any pc, tablet or smartphone right into a digital set top field or streamer, which usually gives users the capacity to flow documents from the web, a typical home network and storage.

On the other hand, the other TV streamers comparable to the brand new Apple tv, and Amazon fire television Stick, Chrome cast 2, Kodi application might not be held back with the aid of a curated app store or licensing, so it allows the users to download a variety of apps, and watch whatever they like.

Chapter 03 – Tips to install Kodi without PC

Kodi is the most fantastic method to stream the material to the television from a pc or phone, and utilizing Android television is the high quality strategy to turn your "dumb" television in to the smart one.

Whilst the streaming of the application of Kodi to Chrome cast is a bit of problematic, getting Kodi onto the Nexus participant, Android television or Nvidia defend television enabled Sony, Sharp TVs, or Philips is the complete doddle. Here is how one can get Kodi installed in your Android television and streaming the users stored content material onto the large reveal.

There are two approaches to stream content material from the Kodi application to Android television. The procedure is to utilize the Chrome cast performance and circulate Kodi through Chrome cast. Nevertheless, the opposite direction is very less difficult that it may endorse the user not to even waste their time looking to fiddle around with Chrome cast.

Installing Kodi the highly easy manner:

1. Download the application of Kodi to the television of Android.
2. Configure the application of Kodi to peer the content that the user might have saved on to the network.
3. Ended.

Mounting Kodi the long winded method:

For some of the most important reasons, the user cannot download Kodi from the Google Play retailer, the following points shows the different strategy to download it onto your Android television.

1. Open the Settings of Android television panel and scroll to protection and Limitations.
2. Activate the Unknown Sources to allow for set up of application and software outside of the Play store of Google.
3. Install and Download the application of Kodi for Android from download page of Kodi – also depending for the hardware, the user needs to choose for both the x86 variant and ARM.
4. Make the copy of the downloaded the file of extension .apk to the drive or a USB drive and after that plug it into the Android television.
5. Navigate to where the user may store the file of extension .apk using ES File Explorer or the different file administration application.
6. Open the file of extension .apk to be asked in the event that the user may be like to install Kodi and pick the option of "set up".
7. As soon as the file has accomplished transferring throughout to the machine, the user might be asked as soon as once more when the user may like to place in Kodi. Choose the option of "set up".
8. Kodi will set up and work precisely as if it would be once downloaded from the Play store of Google.
9. Organize Kodi so the user may going to find the content the user may going to have saved within the network.
10. Completed.

On the other hand, the other TV streamers comparable to the brand new Apple tv, and Amazon fire television Stick, Chrome cast 2, Kodi application might not be held back with the aid of a curated app store or licensing, so it allows the users to download a variety of apps, and watch whatever they like.

Installing Kodi on Chrome Cast:

Download show settings and be certain exhibit hidden records are ticked.After that, make sure that the Kodi or XBMC media center is linked to the Kodi application. As soon as performed, go into ES File Explorer once more and open the folder of Downloads. Right here the user will have to find the Factory Core Player .Xml file that the user may downloaded earlier (if not, navigate to where his downloaded records were previously stored). Make copy of knowledge and look for either org .Xebec .Kodi or "org. Xebec. And .Xebec files dependent on which streamer the user may utilize. Kodi would be "org .Xebec .Kodi" as soon as open, click through files .Kodi (or .Xebec, relying user data and then paste the Factory Player Core .Xml file into the folder. Open the application of Kodi and navigate it on to the file of that the user may need to observe. The application Kodi will then robotically launch Local Cast and although Android will ask the user which application of casting may wish to use. Once loaded, the user will be precipitated to press the play and asked which device the user may need to prefer to move to. The user then ought to click on to the option of Play an additional time, and it must, ultimately, play on to the Chrome cast-related television.

Kodi application runs on any pc, tablet or smartphone right into a digital set top field or streamer, which usually gives users the capacity to flow documents from the web, a typical home network and storage.

Chapter 04 – Tips to Install Kodi on the Chrome Cast

Kodi and the Chrome cast are ultimate companions. One of the most important piece of streaming application the user could get, the opposite is the pleasant streaming dongle cash can purchase – collected they make a killer bundle for the close streaming to anything the user wish to have it for their smart TV.

You most common learn about Kodi and its advantage, particularly for those users who like watching TV programs, movies or streaming live activities and programs. Considering Kodi is the most important and open source application, it can be installed on just about any device and is infinitely moldable so that the user could customize it to fit the desires exactly – or download a build which anybody else has made in the users wants. Whilst that user may put Kodi application on whatever the user adore, media streamers are one of the crucial most flexible and lightweight methods to get Kodi content on to the television. Google's new 4K Chrome cast extremely, its average Chrome cast or fire television of Amazon's Stick all provide low cost and effortless approaches to create a dedicated, transportable Kodi computing device.

But then again how does the user go about getting the application of Kodi onto his Amazon fireplace TV Stick or Chrome cast? Much Thankful, it is now not that much tricky and now we have gone through the method for downloading the application of Kodi on Chrome cast under so that the users are able to do the same too. If some of the users wish to find out how they can set up the application of Kodi on Amazon fireplace TV stick, they can easily navigate there utilizing the record on to the left field.

Before beginning to download the Kodi on chrome cast, you don't have to move Kodi content material to Chrome cast from the device of an iOS, so it will be best about the tools of Android for this procedure. There are two main approaches that the user may need for having the content to Chrome cast from their Kodi related Android tools: the lengthy, yet vigor friendly method; but battery intensive, or the quick, route.

The Long Method:

1. Download show settings and be certain exhibit hidden records are ticked.
2. After that, make sure that the Kodi or XBMC media center is linked to the Kodi application.
3. As soon as performed, go into ES File Explorer once more and open the folder of Downloads.
4. Right here the user will have to find the Factory Core Player .Xml file that the user may downloaded earlier (if not, navigate to where his downloaded records were previously stored).
5. Make copy of knowledge and look for either org .Xebec .Kodi or "org. Xebec. And .Xebec files dependent on which streamer the user may utilize. Kodi would be "org .Xebec .Kodi" as soon as open, click through files .Kodi (or .Xebec, relying user data and then paste the Factory Player Core .Xml file into the folder.
6. Open the application of Kodi and navigate it on to the file of that the user may need to observe.
7. The application Kodi will then robotically launch Local Cast and although Android will ask the user which application of casting may wish to use.
8. Once loaded, the user will be precipitated to press the play and asked which device the user may need to prefer to move to.
9. The user then ought to click on to the option of Play an additional time, and it must, ultimately, play on to the Chrome cast-related television.

The Short Method:

1. Open the application of Chrome cast in the Android gadget.

2. Click on the menu and decide upon the option of cast screen / audio alternative and try to follow all the guidelines to hook up with the Chrome cast.
3. Open the application of Kodi.
4. If the user may try to find the video, he / she may want to watch and press the icon of play.
5. It would be playable on across both of the gadgets, but that user would be able to turn their display off or take calls.

Tips to install Kodi on a Chrome cast by making use of a laptop

Streaming XBMC or Kodi content material to a Chrome cast from a pc would not be as difficult as the user may also feel; however – like streaming Android content – it would be a long way from the stylish strategy to the users' main issue.

1. Download Chrome and the application of Chrome cast, ensuring the user may have a Kodi or XBMC customer hooked up on your laptop.
2. Download the Chrome and its application Chrome cast for casting the extension.
3. Open Chrome and prefer the "cast" alternative out of the users' Chrome cast extension.
4. The place that the users may see on the option of cast this tab to may have right and can be a small down arrow, click on this option and decide upon the cast complete monitor.
5. As soon as it is carried out, the users entire laptop desktop should be streaming to their television.
6. Open XBMC or Kodi and fan the flames of a video to watch.

Chapter 05 – The Best Kodi Addons and Kodi Builds

If the user want to watch a variety of game and films, or movies he/she will surely love Kodi. XBMC or Kodi is a streaming application that lets the user to watch whatever he wants whether it is in the community retailer on a hard force, or on the web. Kodi is the most important open source application, and that suggests it may be adapted and tailor-made to fit your wants – and there would be an enormous variety of addons that can help you do that.

Whether or not the user may want to entry his/her Netflix account, hearken to the radio or watch anime – there would be the Kodi extension always available for its users. To make matters much simpler, the developer put collectively the names of the first-class thirteen first rate Kodi add-ons in the November 2016.

1. Channel Prime wire

The extension of the 1Channel Prime wire is the most notable Kodi add-ons in the year of 2016, and that is considering the fact that it elements are everything. Actually, if the user is no longer too afflicted about modifying Kodi, the 1Channel Prime wire would – alongside Specto or Exodus is some of the simplest addons the user may want.

2. Specto

Specto is the beginning adds on resuscitated and up to date for the year of 2016, comprehensive with the other links. Just as the origin before it, Specto is now has the most essentially and the high quality collection of URLs and links, so that the user could circulate television programs and movies compatible for the entire household.

Therefore, need to download the enormously viewed Kodi addons in a brand new, refreshed kind.

3. Exodus

Genesis was once the finest addons that the user would be available for Kodi application, but in view that then content have engaged a try for the more serious – links fitting common. Exodus created by way of the developer of Genesis, the application of Exodus is one of the widespread addons on hand for Kodi application – and the customers or Kodi are already announcing it is probably the most exceptional.

4. Velocity

Velocity signifies one of the most up-to-date, exceptional add-ons for both the Kodi and XBMC, but it is surely already proving much notable functions. Since it could be handy to make use of and carries with it a number of novel content material and accelerated control. It additionally has two approaches, so there is a speed kid's variation for smaller users of Kodi too.

5. Salts

It is developed by using the identical persons that introduced the SALTS and 1channel.Ch stands for circulate the entire Sources and that explains the users generally all they have got to understand. By this time tipped as a pleasant alternative to the Genesis, the application of SALTS is quick, convenient to make use of and is not much difficult to install.

6. Phoenix

Another addons which is named as Phoenix needs to be at the first and foremost of any addons' lists. The developers of Mash up made up the – beforehand probably the most satisfactory addons for Kodi or XMBC – and maintained by way of a committed crew of builders, Phoenix lets his users to watch whatever the user may want to in much high quality. It may takes few minutes or seconds to get installed, and will also let the user decide on their bit expense in case the user have a frail link.

Best Kodi Builds:

Following are the best Kodi Builds:

1. Nemesis

In case the user may after the neat, high quality construct for Kodi, the user could do inferior than Nemesis. Providing to its users the whole favorite add-ons comparable to cartoon HD that are capable to move, Nemesis makes use of a clean, functional interface that runs good on almost whatever. Due to the three line menu procedure, it would be effortless to pass straight to the content or add-ons the user may want, that means which the user can get streaming as quickly as viable.

2. Apollo

Without any difficulty, the Apollo is among the best builds that the user may get on Kodi application now. It uses a personalized skin so the user interface best, however dig deeper and the user would be in finding the entire addons that user might want – and a many other things. Regardless of its nature, the Apollo is without a doubt very steady, so whether or not the user may on a low-powered desktop or a fire TV Stick, the user must not expertise many crashes either.

3.   *Evolution*

In the event the user may after whatever the looking than the ordinary Kodi construct the technique of Evolution would the Kodi build for its users? Established on the futuristic Arctic Zephyr skin and ethereal, Evolution looks first rate – and is much equally agreeable to its use. Like the other builds, Evolution is the entire most notable Kodi add-ons, however makes a specialty of family entertainment, which means that the user would be able to keep the whole attention of its users.

Conclusion:

Kodi application runs on any pc, tablet or smartphone right into a digital set top field or streamer, which usually gives users the capacity to flow documents from the web, a typical home network and storage. Kodi is the most high quality portions of streaming software in the market place in the present time. Kodi is the most important open source application, and that suggests it may be adapted and made to fit the users' wants – and there would be an enormous variety of addons that can help the user do that. Kodi and the Chrome cast are ultimate companions. If some of the users wish to find out how they can set up the application of Kodi on Amazon fireplace TV stick, they can easily navigate there utilizing the record on to the left field. Kodi is the notable application for streaming live the videos or other digital media files in the present time. Now it only helps the users to stream content to their television through practically internet related device, but also the application is the open source in nature and is highly customizable. Kodi is the most high quality application also for streaming software in the present market. Kodi is extremely and easily customizable application.

FREE Bonus Reminder

If you have not grabbed it yet, please go ahead and download your special bonus report *"DIY Projects. 13 Useful & Easy To Make DIY Projects To Save Money & Improve Your Home!"*

Simply Click the Button Below

OR **Go to This Page**

http://diyhomecraft.com/free

BONUS #2: More Free & Discounted Books or Products

Do you want to receive more Free/Discounted Books or Products?

We have a mailing list where we send out our new Books or Products when they go free or with a discount on Amazon. Click on the link below to sign up for Free & Discount Book & Product Promotions.

=> Sign Up for Free & Discount Book & Product Promotions <=

OR Go to this URL

http://zbit.ly/1WBb1Ek